THE LANDLADY
IN BANGKOK

The National Poetry Series

The National Poetry Series was established in 1978 to publish five collections of poetry annually through five participating publishers. The manuscripts are selected by five poets of national reputation. Publication is funded by the Copernicus Society of America, James A. Michener, Edward J. Piszek, the Lannan Foundation, and the Andrew W. Mellon Foundation.

1993 COMPETITION WINNERS

The Other Man Was Me: A Voyage to the New World,
by Rafael Campo
      Selected by Gloria Vando. Arte Publico Press.

The High Road to Taos, by Martin Edmunds
      Selected by Donald Hall. University of Illinois Press.

The Landlady in Bangkok, by Karen Swenson
      Selected by Maxine Kumin. Copper Canyon Press.

The Other Stars, by Rachel Wetzsteon
      Selected by John Hollander. Viking Penguin.

Most Way Home, by Kevin Young
      Selected by Lucille Clifton. William Morrow & Co.

THE NATIONAL POETRY SERIES
SELECTED BY MAXINE KUMIN

The
Landlady
in Bangkok

KAREN SWENSON

COPPER CANYON PRESS

ported by a grant from the National
grant from the Lannan Foundation.
Canyon Press has been provided by
tion, the Lila Wallace–Reader's Digest
te Arts Commission. Copper Canyon
rum at Fort Worden State Park.

of Sakyamuni Buddha. Pala style,
12th century. Courtesy of Chidori Antiques, Seattle, Washington.

Library of Congress Cataloging in Publication Data

Swenson, Karen, 1939–

The Landlady in Bangkok: poems / by Karen Swenson.
p.   cm.
ISBN 1-55659-067-9
I. Title.
PS3569.W39L36 1994
811'.54–DC20   94-9843
CIP

COPPER CANYON PRESS
PO BOX 271, PORT TOWNSEND, WASHINGTON 98368

FOR PETER
who believes that women and birds should wing it.

FOR WILLIAM MATTHEWS
AND EDMUND PENNANT
over many years staunch and sumptuously giving friends.

Table of Contents

Acknowledgments

I would like to thank Yaddo and the Albee Foundation
where many of these poems were written and revised.

Blue Unicorn: "Three Silences in Thailand"
Calliope: "The Ghost"
Caprice: "Alien Women: Songkhla, Thailand"
Confrontation: "Uncoupling in Bali"
Denver Quarterly: "The Landlady in Bangkok," "Trekking
   the Hills of Northern Thailand"
Georgia Review: "We"
Michigan Quarterly: "The Garden"
Mudfish: "The Cambodian Box"
Pequod: "The Guide"
Pivot: "Manokwari, Irian Jaya"
Prairie Schooner: "The Bracelet," "Bayon," "Market
   Women," "Getting a Purchase"
Prospect Review: "Hybrids of War"
Salmagundi: "The Beast"
Southern California Anthology: "The Angel of Death
   in Sumatra"
Southern Poetry Review: "Cold Blood," "Adam and His
   Father," "Medias Res"

THE LANDLADY
IN BANGKOK

Consider my traveling expenses:
Poetry –
all of it
is a journey to the unknown.

"Conversation with a Tax Collector about Poetry"
VLADIMIR MAYAKOWSKI

PRELUDE

What Does a Woman Want?

We read the same books as children – Kipling,
Haggard, Stevenson – and dreamt adventure,
but they went off, the boys, to munch on sago
grubs with cannibals, be rocked to sleep

in a hold where rats and roaches rustled
under the slap of a moon-starched sail
and on the volcano's steaming lip, pose
for the camera, their calves fringed with leeches.

Coming to adventure late I'm not sure
I'd savor grubs. I didn't join my Burmese
bus companions when they dined with their
right hands. On a tramp off Sumatra's coast,

I held a scream, a bobbing bathtub toy
in my throat, as two-inch roaches filed
above my head. My bones ached to the marrow
scrambling up to fourteen thousand feet.

I envy the acceptance that accrues to cocks.
They are the universal, catholic sex.
Witch doctors don't ask wives why they've allowed
their husbands out to roam the world alone.

Green with begrudging as a young rice field,
I'm a prurient curiosity,
in my unorthodox sex, to the local men
in foreign towns who hope, or else assume.

7

They're shoals to navigate with care as I
tack Malacca's strait, round Java's head
sails spread and bellying to cross the shadow
line, gathering my way before the salty wind.

BURMA

The use of traveling is to regulate imagination
by reality, and instead of thinking how things
may be, to see them as they are.

SAMUEL JOHNSON

Cold Blood

After murdering his father
and marrying all the widows,
King Narathu feared reincarnation.
Perhaps he'd return as a lizard
to be stoned by the villagers,
skinned and roasted –
a sputtering drizzle of juice in the fire.

To evade fate he built
the largest temple in Pagan
on the plain already a hummocked quilt
of mud brick bribes against mortal deeds.

Mornings, he trailed his courtiers behind him
like a child with a clacking pull-toy,
through the dusty bristle of palms,
to insert a needle between yesterday's bricks.
If he could, the mason lost a finger.

Eight hundred years ago eight assassins
stabbed him, then each other,
but still bricks and mortar –
death's dust steeped and kneaded –
stack neat sandwiches.

In his dim arches, where bats swoop,
we shake our heads over his
litany of iniquity, loving it,

wanting evil to be monstrous, mythical,
something our ordinariness cannot achieve.

When he looked down his tunnel's sealed masonry
to the framed opening of light and green,
perhaps he longed to be
without the dark within.

Emerging from his shadows
where bats scream at the edge of hearing,
we watch a lizard warm his blood in the dust
circled by boys,
pouches of slingshots pulled taut
on limber fingers.

The Garden Again

The Romans, retreating from the wilderness
of Britain four centuries after Christ,
left mosaic faces laced grey with lichens,
left their stones, dressed and ordered
as soldiers in the rain.

In downtown Rangoon,
a leftover edifice of empire
sprouts trees from its Victorian brick
while a mile away crowds swirl colors skirting
the gilded pinnacles of the Shwedagon pagoda.
In the countryside,
the woven bamboo houses pour
dust-brown children from window and door
surrounding a church's brick fortress where
swifts skim through windows stained only by sunset.

At the end of sovereignty, just as the sea
gardens a wreck with coral and anemones,
the emptiness of empire fills up,
a compost of leaves and wings.

The Beast

The teak is carved, fine as mantilla lace,
dark with alien iconography.
Rummaging for a familiar shape,
among the forms that climb each other's backs
like acrobats beneath the Burmese sun
I ask, "That carving, is that a beast who's
carrying a woman in his hairy arms?"
Among gilded temples I am told this tale:

>"The King, only a daughter to his name, calls
>astrologers, a colloquy of beards, to
>foretell the fate they read within her face.
>'She will be seized by eagle talons,' they say.
>He builds a platform far from where birds nest
>and orders guards to shoot all that fly near.

>"The bleached bones of ten years of wings now
>   bracelet
>where she, more beautiful each year, strokes sparks
>like crackling stars from the dark of her hair.
>Of course, one day an eagle in a storm sweeps
>down a thunderbolt, and she is gone
>beyond both town and river of the kingdom.

>"He drops her carelessly as any fate;
>she falls a dark-haired comet through the sky,
>through open arms of branches to the forest floor.
>The ogre, hunting roe deer, finds her lying
>among leaves bright with the berries of her blood

and lifts her head's dark burden to his breast.

"He nurses her to health and to his love,
conceals his fanged mouth and his feral eyes
with charms that cast him bright and princely
into her sight, but when their child is born
he will not stand before his son's eyes knowing
there is no spell to hide you from your blood.

"The astrologers, their beards a decade longer,
inform the King he has a living daughter
and heir beyond the river in the forest.
The King sends soldiers. Hastening with her son –
her husband's gifts of bangles gild her arms –
she leaves behind a message with her love.

"The ogre, stumbling in his fear of loss,
forgetting any incantations but
the names of his loves, follows them and calls,
and calls right to the river bank. His son,
in terror of the strange pursuing beast,
draws his bow and strikes his father's heart.

"Lips twisted to a grimace by his fangs,
the ogre's head lies at his wife's small feet
who in disgust at this grotesque, dead face
furls skirts, contemptuous, over his unfamiliar head
to sail with her son to her father's kingdom."

Gazing at the ogre, dark in his
teak skin, who never risked the generosity
of love and died a stranger, I remember

my Western childhood also had a beast,
but he did not evade his lady's gaze.
She watched him lapping from a pool and offered
his thirst the quenching hollow of her palms.
He drank, as humbly we must all drink from
the cupped hands of love, to change the beast within.

Hatching

For Daw Aung San Suu Kyi

On University Avenue in Rangoon,
each day she dines on solitude.

Made mute by generals,
her voice is amplified by silence.

A bird eats its cell,
to crack its walls with wings.

INDONESIA

Old women ought to be explorers.

AMENDED QUOTE FROM T.S. ELIOT

Orangutan Rehab

A circle of unbarbered redheads round
a blue plastic milk pail hoard bananas
in hairy fists, hold tin cups concentrating –
admonished children wary of spills.

On sultry afternoons, officials teased
these caged exhibits of their power, who
became accustomed to three squares, a roof.

Here, after they've been schooled to make leaf nests,
avoid the poison berry, break
the habit of captivity, they're left in
the jungle – city kids at camp afraid of crickets.

But twice a day they're brought bananas, milk,
until they feed themselves, die of snake bite
or the fall they couldn't have in a cage.

Bananas peeled and stored in her cheek,
she holds by hand and foot to trunk and vine
bombarding me with chunks of termite nest.
That ammunition spent, she craps in her cupped

palm and tries again, observing me
with no more malice than my son japanning
the kitchen wall with pureed sweet potatoes,

then sways as you or I did as a child
from the school jungle gym in a daydream.

A sun shaft haloes carrot red
fur around her skull as she

selects a path, with long arms swings
thirty feet above the ground from limb to
limb toward a cultivated taste for freedom.

Missionaries

Rusted helmets, dogtags in the garden,
they live in World War Two's abandoned purlieus
under the wave of jungled mountain where
as it crests
a Black Widow fighter shines
in the dark clearing of its crash.

Jungle like green heads of broccoli –
the husbands helicopter over it
to the waiting front line of faith where
headmen squat on naked haunches
wearing necklaces of safety-pins,
while wives drink tea,
embroider, knit or nurse a twelve-year-old

through quinine visions in late afternoon
heat tremors, and screams of white cockatoos,
until dinner reassures with flavors
from freezers stacked with
hamburger and cupboards stocked
with peanut butter, and Spam.

At a bonfire of the fetishes,
husbands stir the ashes of their godly
war glinting with the cowrie eyes of charred
idols, spoils of faith.
Led by wives, a Pentecostal flock at prayers
purls like cramped chickens.
Retreating from ancestral forests to

the neutral zone of Christ, this unprotected
species marches narrow halls of psalms,
Stone Age refugees redeemed from fire
of government
helicopter gunships to learn
how to iron their new white shirts.

Manokwari, Irian Jaya

In Memoriam, Alfred Russel Wallace

Dangling rainbows of skipjack swing
from poles on shoulders of peddlers.
Housewives with crossed arms breathe the cool
morning at their open, hill-perched doors.

Calling *selamat* to them softly,
I look from road to the blue, calm bay –
first harbor of Dutch missionaries,
Wallace's fever-misted anchorage.

Outriggers ride, waterstriders at rest;
the monthly freighter drowses at the pier.
Above, beyond its barren spars, the Arfak
mountains blue horizons burdened with cloud.

I turn from sun into an apse of jungle.
The path, a century of leaves makes spongy
footing, is hung with bare
thread-tapestries, a spider crouched in each.

As Darwin traced our sandy prints backward from
shore into water, Wallace, looking forward,
tracked our spoor of animal graves to
the future – animals we've sung and painted.

Listen. A pair of fantails,
wings lost in green domes, drop triads

of clarinet notes, globes that plummet air
plangent in the jungle silence.

A bare beginning of a melody which, beyond
the curtain of leaves in the man-made
kingdom, Mozart might have played, a grace
of notes, a little twilight music.

Stalking Lemurs

4 A.M., the moon down world is dark
as the river's black volcanic bed
outside my bamboo door. A knock wakes me.
Fumbles of shoelaces, flashlight, clothes. I enter
the night escorted by the river's
invisible sibilants, track my guide's heels over
stumbles of roots with my flashlight's circle
until we must walk without it.

In the jungle's moist shroud, surrounded by bat
shrill gossiping we breathe the dark. A flick
of flashlight spots the copper-penny eyes;
spidery fingers clasp a branch.
Among trees hung with watchful gleams my guide
and I, compassed by our illumination, are
bound by family resemblances
to these hands and faces vanishing
into leaves and dawn.

Sulawesi: Balconies of the Dead

Islands of trees hummock up in green
paddies shading lean-tos grey as mud
crusted buffalo. Above, the broken
teeth of limestone cliffs gape with rain-carved
caves, stone mouths in which the dead are stored.
The new in pig-shaped coffins lie among
the last generation's skull-rubble.
A row of men and women, effigies
set with moonshine, mother-of-pearl eyes,
stand at the cave's lip, their travel bags,
filled with the necessities of death,
slung over wooden shoulders. Hands at rest on
the balcony fence, they're vacationers
ready to wave from a cruise ship's rail.
They gaze down into the living
theater of seed and scythe while those
who plant lean on a plow to squint through sun
up at the audience of the dead.

The Angel of Death in Sumatra

Exotic is our mutual word in the village
of thatched roofs swept up into horns,
yet its yards, brown with drying cloves, are
the fragrance of childhood toothache cures

and snow-hushed nights that steamed with mulled
    red wine.
Women invite from doorways, offer food,
children follow astonished that I'm amazed by
the monotony of every day.

Giggling at each other, we turn the corner
of a house crouched beneath its shaggy thatch
to be silenced by an old man's hammer
nailing boards to shape a small box.

Nothing's more ordinary or amazing
than the coffin he lines with black plastic.
In America we'd tuft pink satin
and make-believe a bassinet.

The children and I are respectful, solemn
before its void. In a placenta shroud,
the shape beside the box is smaller than
a pillowcase of laundry. I wonder

at the angel, skin brown as oiled walnut,
sarong tight under her wings, trailing the black
thistledown of her hair past volcanoes

garnished with cloud, who looked down

at the humped Brahmin cows – cream clotted against
the valley's green. Perhaps descending into
the delicate scent of cloves, which for her was
unstained with red wine or remembrance

of childhood pain, she felt an awkwardness
that without any experience of flesh,
not even a sense of smell, she should have such
intimate, such carnal knowledge of us.

Market Women: Lake Toba

They've come on board their grocery baskets full
to gossip and shake off the clinging sand
from bare feet and vegetables. They pull
weeds from pale tails of beansprouts as we land.
These women then will disappear
into their lives. But now I can watch them,
the ordinariness of their day, sheer
exotica. That word's apothegm
is their sarong-wrapped squat embellished by
a wilderness of *batik* birds and blooms
while we, another clan in our blue Levis,
our dungaree and sneaker tribal costumes,
feed their curiosity's appetite,
our differences our mutual delight.

The Bracelet

Two days I bargained over this brass round
of beasts that, breaching from each other, ring
my wrist. A man at a *batik*-stall frowned,
admiring his tribe's artistry, the sting
of loss in his smile, as he congratulated
me on my low price. Without understanding
the myths, it bought the bronze curve they created.
The Mobil-oil wife guides her in-laws on blue
Lake Toba while the ferry's decibels
of sixties-rock drown her captions on the view,
her news that all the tribes were cannibals
before the Dutch converted them. "The crew,"
she tells me, "don't seem to mind being poor,
not at least the way we would mind, for sure."

The Balinese Witch Doctor

He sits in the circle of his simmering
pressure lamp. (First you must find its private sound.)
Outside the compound's wall, frogs ribbit in the moon
silvered paddies. (Its own combination of
vowels and consonants.) Night after night he studies
the thin palm-leaf books of grandfather, father (because
evil answers to its name), the mantras, the etched
drawings, clues to a new demon generation
of poisons, killers rising from mosquito coils,
the sweet perfume mist of insecticides.

Under frangipani's pinwheel blooms
(you call evil like a dog) he's spent the day
on fortunes told to giggles of girls, charms composed
to banish roaring spirits from dreams, water blessed
to rinse away witch-spelled insanity (and it
obeys, begs, sits, plays dead), he listens to his grand-
    daughter
sleeping in rough bouts of breath between her parents.
He scours for the demon, labors for her breath,
while on the family altar the down on a headless
baby chicken stirs in moonlight's shadows.

Uncoupling in Bali

I.

Playing with the mystery of distance
in your binoculars, the witch doctor
inquires about your two most puzzling
behaviors – "Why you look birds?" "Why you let
woman travel lone?" You wing your hands,
a visual aid. "Free," you say, "Bird. Woman,"
and smile beneath the hover of your hands.

II.

The evening after you leave me I sit
as we have each dusk to watch the swifts dart
in near collision, arcing their aerial dance
on boomerang wings over the ripe whisper
of paddies, but not one pair comes to skim
the dark air. I wait. The moon arrives
to thumbprint the night sky with mercury.
Someday one of us will be returned,
from this middle-aged romance, to loneliness.

The Dutchman in Bali

Split, the babe in Solomon's judgment,
between the claims of Klungkung and Rotterdam,
forty homeless years bring him back
to bloody betel splashes in the market dust.
The women look up from their old sarongs
spilled with papayas, to speak
his language softly from their childhood.
They are the home that he was exiled from.

Men leave their rice to keep his pace
along green ridges of their paddy dikes
and take their foreign grandpa's hand.
Their bowdlerized memory recalling only
the peace and order of the Dutch.

Battered children who insist
they had a happy family, they've forgotten
processions in white garments of death, thousands
charging to their suicide with jeweled *krises*
under muzzles of Dutch guns.
He returns to shiver in Rotterdam,
blood colonized by his lost childhood's warmth.
His doctors prescribe penicillin for his homelessness.

No Exemption for Tourists

A foreign family –
mother, father,
ten-year-old daughter –
stroll through the lush spill
of green, chambered
with voices of grasshoppers and frogs,
savoring the fastidious sensation
of being a unique unit
in an otherwise homogeneous landscape,
the tourist feeling that life
has suspended its rules
and the world has become a petting-zoo.

They pause to watch, where the path
skirts the fall of paddy terraces,
darting scarlet dragonflies
sizzle air on gold netted wings
and figures working around
two mounds below.
The bank is blocked
by turns in the path,
green paddles of banana leaves,
as voices become
more distinct, chiming
in and out of the river's sound.

Rounding the last corner
they come out
at the river bank,

at the two mounds –
two bodies soaking
through their shrouds
improvised from flowered sarongs.
A woman, snail tracks of tears
on her cheeks, urges them back.
"Suicide.
Girl, boy,"
she explains in English.
The parents move their bodies
in front of their daughter,
turn her up the hill.
"Disgusting," she says.
They chatter the day's cheerful plans
over her head –
a pair of birds
weaving a protective nest of words –
while green rice bends down
to the bright ribbon of river.

Isn't It Romantic?

The guide book promised birds of paradise,
impenetrable jungle, semi-nude tribes,
palm-leaf huts wafting their fringed eaves.

I've got mosquito netting clotted with dust,
large bugs in a cold shower, plentitudes
of naked scrotums posing for my camera.

If I cancel my appointments with
the mummified chief smoked by village elders
and the brine pool across the woven-vine bridge,

I could spend the day on postcards and
pretend I'm talking to my friends surrounded
by village idlers in penis gourds and grass skirts

who pass round the postcards pointing out
the sites of their lives, while loneliness,
a drying rawhide noose, strangles my spirit.

Mother's hand is lost in Woolworth's for eternity.
I long for my personal helicopter to
whirl me from this place I most wanted to be.

Cultural Exchange

For Madonna

I.

In the cave of movie-house fictive dark,
he watches flickers of another life.

Equatorial heat macerates the afternoon streets.

Pale men, guns held at cock level
spew fire. Their enemies jerk-dance,
leaves in a typhoon.

The clerk puts away fake trading beads for tourists.

But it is the woman he waits for
the woman unlike his yam-planting wife
who turns her body over to him reluctantly
as she delivers the pig for butchering.

Shop shutters close on axes chipped from soft, grey stone.

The man grabs her.
The pale woman moans.
Hips thrust.
The man throws her
to the floor.

Who knows the old axes, the real ones?

He follows the camera's dismembering eye:
the gasping mouth
the breasts creaming over undone buttons
the rucked-up skirt.
She absorbs the man
a drought field taking in rain, content.

They took patient weeks to chip from hard, green stone.

II.
In my dining room
outside the lamp's circle

>over the river's tumult of muddy foam
>the bridge

beyond the table's conversation
among half-empty glasses   crumpled napkins

>suspends its web of vines and sticks
>the man appears
>on the path

at the edge of the embrace
of friends' laughter   questions

>on the narrow path
>I scramble
>through brush
>snarls of long grass

Aren't you afraid
a woman traveling

A Walk with Shadows in the Bada Valley

He knew in kindergarten he would serve
the Lord, the missionary pilot from
that flat world of Ohio. He lands me,
beneath the jungled mountain's mossy curve,
into this world brought to Christendom
but known for stone faces at crossroads
or among the heavy heads of rice –
large-eyed statues orphaned by their makers
who left, disappearing into death.

In a house edging a dirt path that rambles
the valley, a boy lays out in the pressure
lamp's light, postcards of New York and glossy
samples of my family. In exchange
he offers me an album, turns with grave pride

the pages' Kodacolor promenade –
snapshots of a boy his age with ruler
parted hair in a First Communion suit
arranged on satin in front of a brigade
of relatives whose heads are bowed in prayer.

Following their grief-taut faces through
the sermon, hymns, the walk behind the box,
I stand on the raw dirt edge with these few
listening to the thud of the first
clods on the lid of hope. He shuts the album.

The lonely monoliths, abandoned when
their makers wandered off the path of time
into the fields of eternity,
come to people my dreams. From where they
guard crossroads or are nestling rain-wracked cheeks
in green rice, they come to peer into the black box.
The pilot, meanwhile, out of gas in his
Savior Cessna, weeps and can't lift off.

Medias Res

The middle's where I wonder why as I wake
and shake a roach, size of a half-smoked stogie,
from my backpack to the jungle. I'm the pale
anomaly, new mushroom species, sprouting
among the women on the bamboo platform
who suckle babies or coil up hair lustrous
as hot tar. In knee-high mud socks, they stroll
downhill from mired Jeeps to bathe. I follow,
slithering. Men heave and haul a dozen trucks
up switchbacks grey with elephant hide mud.
All day eating canned Australian cheese or
searching for a private place to pee
while idle men follow me in the hope
men hope about all foreign women, I wonder why.

The last truck hauled, the jungle night's quick shutter
closes. The Jeep accelerates its shriek
up switchbacks, headlights extracting objects from
the night – mud ruts, a palm hairnetted with vines
looming at cliff edge, snailed fiddleheads
of tree ferns embedded in this dinosaur dark,
articulate with a wild vocabulary
of greens – Nile, absinthe, cucumber, jade, parrot.
The Jeep stops to let a truck strung with colored
lights like a Las Vegas chorine churn past.
Blindfolded by night, my ears are impaled
by the shrieking rabble of cicadas,
whose eyes are invisible except in
imagination, I wonder knowing why.

Wedding Bed in Mangkutana

In the village guesthouse
it fills the room it stands in,
a statement of human
belief in idyllic desire.

Curlicued rills of wrought iron
are festooned with lace mosquito net
thrown back from its dark, welcoming cave
where the conjunction of improbabilities occurs –
a boy, knowing cows and goats, is
to be patient, tender;
a girl, a childbirth witness, is
to be responsive, passionate.

From this seed bed, despite
withered harvests, children dead of malaria,
on sheets and pillows strewn
with dainty confetti of embroidered flowers,
belief would have desire
sprout itself out of spit and semen
flourish taller than stunted tapioca and corn
from the same soil.

MALAYSIA

Allah has laid out the earth for you like a vast
carpet so that you will travel its endless roads.

THE KORAN

The English Graveyard in Malacca

Downhill from the roofless Portuguese cathedral
these aliens, from the opposite point of the compass,
lie, a community in the grass, insular
under a great tree's shade by the sea.

Nancy Henry, David Kidd, Lieutenants White and
Harding, Rachel Milne, whose husband translated
the Bible into Chinese – confusing local certitudes –
abandoned by both God and Empire, please

only the wanton grass. A Nissan paint can is
today's descendant of the vases which have held
a century of flowers for the spirit
of the tree that spreads its shade across their clay.

Share Taxi to Singapore

"You living Hollywood?"

> The old woman's *durians*,
> hedgehogs in a canvas sack, lurch
> over my feet as she and I
> and the young man slither into
> each other's sweating arms and thighs.

"New York near Hollywood?"

> One fellow-passenger wears jeans,
> a tech-school shirt sheetmetal stiff
> with starch, but his eyes are full of
> flares as a philosopher
> beaming in on an ideal.

"But you go Hollywood?"

> Fastening on my smile, in lieu of
> seatbelt, I imitate
> the grin of the share-taxi's chromium grill
> aimed at oncoming trucks
> that center down this one-lane highway.

"You meet Sly, maybe Raquel?"

> He languishes for Eden and
> a night of stars as we speed past

pale billowed beaches spread with oil
refineries, monkeys playing
grab-tail at the jungle's curb.

THAILAND

Because we leave, things haven't ceased to exist
behind us....

PAUL CLAUDEL
(TRANSLATED BY DAVID ROTHMAN)

The Landlady in Bangkok

Because, separated from us by a language,
we find her a character without a plot,
a cotyledon without an ecosystem,
we invent her a husband, in the alley court,
a barren womb in this quiet cell of Bangkok's hive
under trellised vines in tin cans.

We graft invention on observation,
imagine her dispossessed
by a second wife's fecundity,
while she keeps her clothes in plastic bags
and sleeps upstairs on the corridor floor
before doors of the Spartan rooms she rents us.
We pass on hypotheses with other travelers' news –
names of hotels in Burma,
prices of guides in Borneo.

We know she counts herself to sleep with our money,
yet hoards notebooks grinning
with our faces which she forgets
with our comments she can't read.
But her records like our fabrications
are errant gestures around a kind of love.

She has no picture for our words for home
as we've no history for the wheal
of scar raised on her shoulder
as at the temple stairs she
buys piping sparrows in wooden cages

and frees them to gain merit –
each a traveler fluttering
from Samsara to Nirvana.

Fisherman in Songkhla

His mirror shines back with approval, God's
suspense-flick hero. This reborn Alaskan
in his red prophet's beard – the locals think he
may be a Ramayana demon – sweats
his teddy bear belly between the market
stalls where dried fans of fish fins and drapes
of dragonfly-wing silks are on display.
He mutters Biblical quotes, down the aisles, spells
against the customary pagan evils.

For a Nam vet named Jack he tends the grey
rustbucket anchored where the jellybean-colored
trawlers bob in the bay. Told Jack's ship
rescues the boat people, he awaits
his orders tracking little whores who skim
like flying fish from room to room in his
hotel and peppers them with buckshot from Paul
and Revelations while they wonder that
his innocence is as large as his bones.

His God, believing in contagion, proscribes
the houses of all idols. He avoids
the curving roofs of temples and the mansion
turned into a museum where in shadows
of wide eaves generations of the Buddha
are lined up in glass cubicles, and teak
floors shine, polished by bare soles that lived
for centuries upon the other side
of his white coin of history.

By street-lace of evening lights he eats
his shrimp in catsup, sleeps through softly closing
doors of whores to dream he's fishing, hooking
them from their pagan pool. The women gleaming
in their sarongs, the men dark-scaled, pile at
his feet, an offering to God. The Buddhas
in the museum wear the moon's pale garment,
dream of flowers and incense as they hold their
palms open in the gesture of forgiveness.

Alien Women: Songkhla, Thailand

Sun blind in the pharmacy's dim light,
I drift between the glass-topped counters that
display modern panaceas and
dried dosages of Chinese wisdom.

Over fish bones, stag horns, roots I find
almost myself – red hair, myopic eyes,
but Irish and much younger. Her voice a mist
of brogue, she stands, extravagantly pregnant,
a baby's burp stain on her shoulder,

beside her Chinese mother-in-law who
plays twig-fingers on the register's keys.
In this hushed light she's an elder goddess,
Kuan Yin dispensing mercy, eyes dark glints
of pity over cheekbones smudged with age spots.

"Your second?" I ask the daughter-in-law. "Third."
She smiles. "Then life holds few surprises for you."
Considering my commonplace, she gravely
agrees. "That's true." Her mother-in-law's brittle
Chinese fingers count my change.

Both women brought their husbands the rich dowries
of their races' foreign beauty.
They've watched their children building castles
on these alien sands, escaping
from the netted pull of bloodlines.

Together in half-light each is a party
to the coalition of all mothers
without passports or frontiers. I walk
back into the sun's fistful of blades.

Three Silences in Thailand

Beside the Mekong's silt-thick flow
trees studded with flat-leaved epiphytes,
as a woman might weave flowers in her hair,
stretch the languor of their branches
from riverbank to dirt road
but are soundless in my foreign mouth
which has no name to call them.

In the bus station, she and I smile and wait;
she points to my hair, unpins her own
spilling its crow-gloss over her breasts.
Among the shouts of children and blasts of exhaust
I twine her a braid of tactile night.

Confined in the pillar of shadow made by his walls
right palm open, a lotus in his lap,
Wat Si Chum's Buddha smiles from his height.
Lips tranquil as wings at dusk
hover benedictions in the air above.
Knowing only the words for a Christ in pain
I bear no offering but the abstinence of silence.

Jigsaw

A Christian Brother trained, fuzz-cheeked cherub
I didn't fit the social jigsaw. So
at seventeen I fled from Dublin, God,
my family, following the love of my life
to Bangkok's gay bars where queens comb their long
black hair in neoned plate glass mirrors.
Despite the shrieking nights of booze, the black and
blue mornings, I never thought of going home
but found one here. A family of Thais
adopted me – gay's not an awkward piece
in the Thai puzzle. Nights beneath the flame
tree my acquired grandma taught me new words,
even the anachronistic royal
tones, were added on my skein of language 'til over
the phone they couldn't guess my Western face.

Now I'm director of my company,
friends raised among the royal words come to
my Chiang Mai weekend house and I've adopted
my houseboy's children, who mocked me
the day they realized I was a foreigner.
In this land, face, not love sets me, though I'm
a Buddhist and a citizen, apart.

Five years since we cremated my chosen grandma.
The Royal Household lent her a gold coffin;
they sowed her ashes from a Royal gunboat.
Mother, who had wanted a cremation,
we buried so Dad, who'd left forty years back,

would know where to go to grieve. In Dublin
for the funeral, I passed a queen perched
thirty years on the same pub stool who said,
"Haven't seen you in an age," as though
I'd spent a week in London. "Been in Bangkok
screwing charcoal sellers," I said, which
disoriented him from his pink gin.
Traveling between my countries I
consider how I fit in neither, a lost
piece of jigsaw questing for a puzzle.

Background and Design

On TV in a Bangkok shop window,
Michael Jackson is a video
rose centering a ruffled nosegay
of Thai silk frocks. He shifts

like the illusion of black and white tiles
I changed as a child – black on white
to white on black – from ghoul to lover
and back while fantasy battalions

of fiends sprout from manholes and graves.
America's undead armies dance again
in Bangkok following the snake-hip slither
of the dark General and his incandescent eyes.

In their school uniforms a crowd
of brown young faces solemnly watch this one
brown face, a manufacture made
uniform by stardom.

I contemplate my white against
this background and his dark cross
in America as he shifts
from fiend to lover and back.

Polygamy

"When an official goes upcountry
they'll give him anything," she says, this woman
boned like a lark's wing whose feet barely reach
the pedals of the car she's weaving through
the fabric of Bangkok, "their house, their daughter."

She shifts with emphasis. "Particularly
their daughter. It," she pauses on the abstract
pronoun, "breeds a debt the family can
collect. She sang at the hotel in town."
At a light our flanks shudder among

the traffic herd. I see that youthful mistress
smoke-wreathed in rooms of men, sheath her in stoplight
red which cornering like a Ferrari
blinks GO as her soprano flutters mawkish
Thai-pop and rote-learned Beatles vowels.

"My husband, six years later, gave a party
for old employees. He said one would bring
a child. The guests left. The boy stayed." We edge
grey matron Volvo through the poppy and
apricot soiree of triwheeled *tuktuks*.

"I knew. He didn't have to tell." I ask,
"What did you say?" "I said to him, 'I thought you
were different.' But she was young, poor had
to earn her living, while we'd plenty." A bus
bears down. She turns beneath its chromium

grimace into a first wife directing
murmurations of concubine children,
cross-legged obedience at lessons. "Still
I can't forgive. Our daughters are ashamed
and the boy, sixteen now, fails school."

I consider, in Bangkok's weave, what landowner,
fields redistributed by revolution,
does not, passing forfeit hectares in
the moonlight, hear the siren rice call
his name green as unreaped fantasy.

Adam and His Father

Adam's father, always a good provider,
has supplied a childhood of unblemished lawns
perfumed by Sunday barbecues,
catsup and sweet relish –
the only admission of change
the height marks on the kitchen door
and a progression of vehicles – carriage to car.

Adam, at 22, wanders East
where monks robed yellow as October leaves
drift the dawn streets with their begging bowls
and human stinks are quick as rats in the alleys.
Homesick for white bread
he strums "I am a Rock" in Bangkok bars,
buys rice from the dark hands of street vendors.

Adam's father sits in the garden,
evening air thick with honeysuckle
under the gentle shuffle of maple leaves,
and reads letters from Bangkok, Rangoon, Dhaka
in which his son writes,
"Seeing hunger, I know I am hungry.
Perhaps what I have always wanted is to want."

Getting a Purchase

Whoring? I guess I thought it was part
of the adventure, that I was smart to get
sex, interpreter, companion in one
package, but by increments of mornings,
this brown face has grown dear upon my pillow.

Across the jittering spoons on the dining
car table, I watch her laugh at jokes in her
comic book as we ride north to trek the hills.
She won't like that, thinks walking's for the poor,
for farmers and now she's a city lady

who taxis, paints her fingernails. Her father's
a farmer. He sold, first her sister, then her,
to a man from Bangkok when the droughts came.
The two support ten who, in good years, gather
in the rice sheaves, but never enough to buy

back even one. I paid the bar a month's fee.
We went to Koh Samui. Scared, she walked
the beach but wouldn't go into the sea
above her knees unless I held her. We took
the shells she'd chosen in the sand and presents

from Bangkok to the farm. The family was
polite but formal like a nineteenth century crew
lined up to meet the captain's wife who brought
aboard bad luck. She's taught me Thailand, given
me a purchase on the culture, until

she and the country have become a chord
in memory, not separate notes. That body,
each breast sweet as brown domes of the raw sugar
sold in the market, has the softness of
soil clouding round the plow in paddy water.

Two weeks, then I go back to work, to college.
I bought her a diaphragm, urged the pill –
her sister's on her third abortion. Maybe
I can send a small check from time to time.

Felicity

The towels neatly squared along the rod.
My husband's tie plumb underneath his chin.
God = cleanliness and order;
Satan = filth and chaos.
When we were married in the stadium,
a thousand couples uniformly paired –
black-suited grooms and white-frocked brides –
were pleasing to the Lord who with forked lightning,
like the snake's tempting tongue, fights anarchy.
Under His command in our small way, we
contend against the pagans' germs and squalor.

I teach Him and hygiene, not to let
their children swim the *klongs* with gassy floats
of dead dogs. I take clean rice to the old
woman living with quick-slime rats under
the bridge. I tell the twelve-year-old we rescued,
Buddha sold her for her perfect jewel.

Hell is Bangkok, heat, stench, cacophony,
no streets meet at right angles. They've no right
angles in their minds. When my spirit's weak I'll
sit in a gleaming hotel lobby, hushed as
a church (my skin admits me without questions).
Among the tourists purchasing the world
they're used to with their rooms, I've half an hour's
loan of order's bliss, but I've renounced
earth's imitations of God's recompense.

Against the grinning anarchy of Buddhas,
each day I sterilize my path to Him.

The Ghost

Woodsmoke guides us through the mist,
trailing fragrance to
the village. Backpacks, full of conveniences
Western as our beliefs, we're dead set on
finding these people happy
without socks or faucets.

We wear our watches, digital signs
of contamination
by the luminous hands of time.
Like Typhoid Marys we carry progress to
this quietude hoping
here infants have no gene for greed.

Women turn their smiles, shield
children from our cameras
leaving nothing to record but things.
Pictures of palm-frond roofs will slide on our walls
while serious chestnut eyes
must slowly fade on memory's transparency.

My pictures flash upon my wall, bamboo weaves across
my plaster, conjuring up one little Lizu boy
who, transfixed by my repetitive pallor,
pale skin, pale hair, pale eyes,
wept as though he'd met his future's ghost.

The Guide

He leads us to our village destination
through the stubble of forests stolen by
lumber bandits, past bamboo conduits
spilling water down hills to women in
silver and coral necklaces who weave
on backstrap looms while men tend corn and poppies.
His terminus is twenty pipes a night
bought with our fees.

Rising in his beautiful balloon
of opium above his village,
he is transformed
into an East–West Don Juan pursued
by local maidens and Swedish backpackers;
into a Jungle Natty Bumpo, tamer of trumpeting
elephants long dead as these denuded hills,
and as he flatters us older women,
puts flowers in our hair, he letches
not for our pale wrinkles
but for flashlights, watches, jack-knives.

On his morning pipe-dazed path
out of the home odor of woodsmoke,
through the melting shapes of mist
among the stumpy ghosts of jungle, he knows
the culture with the most things wins.

Trekking the Hills of Northern Thailand

The English girl is being sick in the bushes,
helped by the Frenchman.
The American couple are identifying wild flowers.
Our guide is dozing off last night's twenty pipes.

Two pigs squeal in their pen
and the only inhabitant of this abandoned village
comes singing through his nose with a pail full
of corn cobs followed by two blue-eyed kittens.

The jungle's green silence
reoccupies paths where human voices
called each other's names.

Over tattered palm-frond roofs,
over low crests of hills that subside
to the plain's green patchwork of paddies,
sitting on a tree stump, I look out to hills
that answer like an echo these I sit among

and, I suppose, that is all I really want,
the only form of $E=mc^2$ I understand –
file after ragged file of silhouettes,
misty recessions into endless distance–
that there always be other hills.

An American in Bangkok

Perhaps the polluted air
of the city brings it out,
just as strawberries raise up hives
or brandy brings on gout.
A middle-class, rosy, young man,
called Ted, still jet-lagged, knows
why the name of the town's Bangkok.
In a dimly lit dive he acquires
two figures in women's dresses
who blow and roll and leave him
chagrined by remembered caresses.

The knowledge that history's bunk
makes the sum of experience zero.
He buys a blue spoonful of sapphires
which smuggled and resold our hero
intends as his final rebuttal
to prove to his father who's smarter.
But finding they're small, flawed junk,
he hires a threatening thug
who, with refund and gems, absconds
leaving Ted to reflect that the only
honest people are blonds.

Down an alley's crooked elbow he joins
a shirt-tailed circle of men
dealing Eurasian poker.
The antes gulp paper and coins
of value unsure as the proof

of their booze that burns like cayenne.
Waking perfumed by his vomit,
he searches about for his wallet.
How come masterful, white, realistic,
American know-how's misfired?
Still he's optimistic.

Hybrids of War: A Morality Poem

I. *Vietnam*

Shadow cleaves
the cool arcade of tourist
shops from sunlight
as he's severed from the language

of the skin
he shares with buyers
of his ballpoint pens.
A ten-year-old genuine

Norman Rockwell
freckle-faced kid, his mouth
only knows his mother's tongue.
He's a lagniappe from her clientele,

a providence
she sends begging to
fill the rice
bowl broken by his birth.

II. *Cambodia*

Before the rats came,
following the wavering fishline
of her newborn cry,
they found her among pearly slime
of gutted mussel shells,

fish rot, jackfruit rind,
and scabbed plastic in the harbor dump.

Sixteen and solemn,
walled in her street stand's ink perfume
by the gloss of fashionable
faces, as well as *Time* and *Fortune*,
she waits behind the grey
rain-drape of the monsoon
for a face to match her mirror's.

III. *Thailand*

His eyes were made green in
the war that built the Burma Road,
littering dead along its verges –
discarded picnic tins.

The road has also decomposed
into the jungle's root and rains
somewhere north across the river
while here he has imposed

the order of his campaign –
a house, hoed vegetables, petals
English as Michaelmas, their beds
besieged in jungle terrain.

Unslinging packs we rest
among his Western flowers.
Our eyes acknowledge, but don't question,
his within this citadel.

IV. *The Moral*

In a world of face values, what
loyalties have you to this pair,
ally and enemy which war has folded
into the marrow of your bones.

CAMBODIA

Evilness is a specifically *human* phenomenon.

ERIC FROMM

…the feeling of exhilaration which a measure of
danger brings to a visitor with a return ticket.

GRAHAM GREENE

Tuol Sleng:
Pol Pot's Prison

Like photographs of Dutch Schultz which show a slick
haired, ordinary man with unmatched eyes there
is nothing evil in this face. Pol Pot
is a bland, jowly, full-lipped man.
Murder. Torture. Genocide. The big words
leave no mark on this small human face.

His photograph has first place on these walls,
mosaicked with the snapshots of the dead.
Looking into the eye of the camera
their eyes focus down the well of terror –
a child, his upper lip already slashed;
a man grinning madness; a woman blank
faced with one tear, clasps her infant.

In the presence of full face or profile
or candids of the stick-limbed forced to smile up
from beds of torture, I move face to face. My
eyes supersede the camera. Obsessed, I
feel obligated to look one by one,
as though by meeting each pair of eyes
I might....
But all I can do is make them into words.

The Cambodian Box

The silver betel box is formed by two geese
nestled closely as a contented couple
in their silver scallops of feathers.

Empty in the shop window in Bangkok
of all but its beauty,
what household of servants and polished teak
did it belong to
before it came through the jungle in a pocket
to buy a month's rice?

The able hands
brown as bread crusts
that formed this sheen of necks and breasts
are matched by another pair,
the color of rouge,
which practice death's craft
in the paradox of hands
mated perfectly as these shining geese.

Survivors

I.

They came up to her, strangers in the street,
clutched her, dug fingernails into her arm and
told her blond hair, her foreign blue eyes, how their
grandfather was clubbed to death, their child died
of malnutrition, they couldn't find their mother.
Now, she says, ten years later, they are better.

II.

Walled up in the band's riffs of Western rock,
beneath the turning mirror ball that fragments
us into mosaics of faces, we shout
out questions as he watches Vietnamese
bar-girls churn their hips. He yells his wife, his
three daughters tortured, killed. He was in France.
We eat our fish, our chicken, listening to
his family's massacre. His fevered eyes
shine black as lacquerware. We holler our
regrets, our horror. He shrugs and leaves us
for deafness in the rock band's restive din,
for blindness in the glitter of revolving
mirrors, for bar-girls who ask no questions.

One at Play in the Fields of

One came home from forced labor to
collapsed bamboo, leaf rubble of
his village, followed in grief a thread
of happy memory to the field
where, with rice baskets full beneath
silken slaps of Buddhist pennants,
the village picnicked. One found a stench,
putrescent stews of naked women
with their babes in open pits. Now
this one's concierge of the bone tower.

Like Genghis Khan's or Tamerlaine's
skull towers on the wind-raw plains
of Asia, but cooped up in glass,
this is a library of shelved
brain boxes which look out blind to
all compass points for others of their
own kind. I photograph girls labeled
prepubescent, but am tugged to
the next shelf, labeled "Europeans,"
as one nods condolences.

But eyeless, lipless, brought down to bone
I cannot mourn mine separately
since we are every one the dead
as we are every one the killers.
The *longan* tree, rummaging
for bloom and fruit in blood-brewed earth
beneath the pits, one day will shade

picnics, banners, children scratching
games in this dust, at play in
the fields of where we all are one.

Bayon, Angkor Thom

The rise of morning sun sends flights
of scarlet parrots wheeling
in the face of the king who ordered
his features carved as Buddha's.

His complacent smiles are cracked
by root-grips of trees.
The lichens' grey scabs mottle
ruins and trunks
as though they are all the creation
of the same bloody claw.

The morning's first guerrilla shots ring
out over parrot cries. New candidates
for deity, ambush each other before
the millennium of stony smiles.

VIETNAM

For the human soul is virtually indestructible,
and its ability to rise from the ashes remains
as long as the body draws breath.

ALICE MILLER

Time and the Perfume River

Small Buddhas smile above their blooms
on gilded family altars, glide
along the curves of the Perfume,

that river named before the dooms
of war ripped Hue's old gilded hide
and Buddhas' smiles above their blooms.

The river waves are slapping tunes.
Greens sputtering in a wok provide,
along the curves of the Perfume,

the smoke of incense. Children's spumes
of laughter rock small boats whose guide
is Buddha's smile above his blooms.

Those years death rode the river's flume
his rotting incense justified
along the curves of the Perfume

by leaders' greed for power's boom.
War's drowned now in the river's tide
where Buddhas smile above their blooms
along the curves of the Perfume.

My Lai

An embassy's tall gate off a dirt road
is the first anomaly, the second, drinking
tea in a cracked cup, where my people
committed massacre. We walk
to the museum cordoned by eyes
of farmers who live in road dust
as did the dead. My eyes, not meeting
theirs, follow a man, middle-aged now,
once an eighteen-year-old Grunt, and our
woman guide, once a survivor at age six.
We move past dingy exhibits,
a straw hat with a bullet hole,
a basin's chipped white enamel which explain
the dead owned nothing but their lives
whose final moments are blown up on the walls.
The guide, who never meets our eyes, taps
her teacher's wand at each exhibit as
we listen to the glass doors rattled
by the crowd, the windows darkened by their faces.

In a haze of light rain our ex-Grunt squats,
tears pages from his notebook,
folding airplanes for children.
The survivor watches
from the steps of her childhood's museum.
I leave, but these two,
twelve time zones out of twenty-four apart,
are bound in working and in dreaming,
in walking and in eating,

lovemaking and in arguing for the duration
of their lives by what death holds apart.

The Cham Towers at Danang

God-faces that once glared at the sun
have weathered to soft ovals and
eroded rounds, which seem to wait for
a chisel to draw features from stone,
articulate as lovers' lips
murmuring in this tower's shade.

Perhaps the lips the couples use
to kiss are the residual
estate of ancient sculptors worn down
by intermarriage with invaders
until the lineaments of their
inheritance are now long lost.

The farmers burn paper money,
offerings of make-believe rent,
to pay off spirits of landowners
their great-grandparents could not recollect.

We

In a museum of the city
once called Saigon, are snapshots. One's
been blown up so we can all see
it clearly. An American,

a young foot soldier, stands on battle
pocked land, his helmet at a jaunty
tilt, posed for buddies as the Model
Grunt. In his left hand he is dangling,

like Perseus, a head by its hair.
Though not Medusa's, it's his charm
for turning fear to stone. Its stare
will quiet, awhile, his throbbing chest.

The tattered flesh that once dressed collar
bones hangs rags from this Vietnamese
neck, captured with the soldier's scar
of grin by a friend's camera.

Is it enough to see it clearly?
We all know what to think. The whitewashed
walls of a second room show nearly
as many black and white shots of

Cambodian atrocities
against Vietnamese. No room's hung
with what was done to enemies
of Vietnam just as there's no

American museum built
to show off snapshots of My Lai.
One pronoun keeps at bay our guilt
they they they they they they they they.

Book design and composition by John D. Berry, using Aldus Page-Maker 5.0 on an Apple Macintosh iivx. The text type is Linotype's PostScript version of Aldus, designed by Hermann Zapf as a book face to accompany Palatino, and issued by Linotype in 1954; the display type is Ellington, designed by Michael Harvey in the spirit of his hand-lettering on many book jackets, and issued as a digital typeface by Monotype in 1990. Printed and bound by Thomson-Shore, Inc.